D1607225

Forgotten Bible Stories

Margaret McAllister

ILLUSTRATED BY
Alida Massari

LION
CHILDREN'S

Text copyright © 2016 Margaret McAllister
Illustrations copyright © 2016 Alida Massari
This edition copyright © 2016 Lion Hudson

The right of Margaret McAllister to be identified as the author and of Alida Massari to be identified as the illustrator
of this work has been asserted by them in accordance with the Copyright, Designs and Patents Act 1988.

All rights reserved. No part of this publication may be reproduced or transmitted in any form or by any means,
electronic or mechanical, including photocopy, recording, or any information storage and retrieval system, without
permission in writing from the publisher.

Published by Lion Children's Books
an imprint of
Lion Hudson plc
Wilkinson House, Jordan Hill Road,
Oxford OX2 8DR, England
www.lionhudson.com/lionchildrens

ISBN 978 0 7459 6520 8

First edition 2016

A catalogue record for this book is available from the British Library

Printed and bound in China, April 2016, LH06

Contents

Balaam

(pronounced "Baylam")

The people of Israel were on their way from slavery to freedom, from Egypt to the Promised Land. The whole nation was on the move, thousands of them: men, women, children, and all their animals and possessions too. To get to their new home, they had to cross the land of Moab.

BALAK, KING OF Moab, looked out at the throngs of Israelites gathered on the borders of his land. He was terrified. They could completely overwhelm Moab if they wanted to. His only hope was the prophet Balaam, who could bring down a blessing or a curse. Balaam lived a long way off in Amaw, so Balak sent his most important courtiers to Balaam with gifts of money and this message:

"I know that when you curse a people they really are cursed, and if you ask a blessing on them they will receive great blessing. So please, Balaam, come and curse the Israelites for me!"

Balaam wasn't at all sure about this. He knew that God had already blessed the Israelites, and how could he curse what God had blessed? But the king sent more messengers, and finally Balaam realized that King Balak wouldn't take no

for an answer. Reluctantly he saddled his donkey and rode to meet the king.

But Balaam's first thoughts had been right. God didn't want him to curse the Israelites, who were only going to the home he had prepared for them. God sent an angel to stop Balaam – and this is where this story gets a bit strange, because Balaam couldn't see the angel.

The donkey could.

The donkey was very down to earth about this. When it saw a large angel in front of it holding a drawn sword, it quite sensibly tried to get around it by walking through a field. Balaam hit the donkey and made it turn around again.

The angel had disappeared so the donkey walked on until, further along the way, it turned up again. Unfortunately this time they were in a narrow lane with high walls on both sides and no fields to walk through. The donkey did its best by squeezing between the angel and the wall, which meant that Balaam's foot got scraped.

"Ow!" shouted Balaam, and hit the donkey again.

The donkey was not pleased. It had behaved perfectly reasonably and was fed up with Balaam hitting it. Resentfully, it plodded on.

When the angel appeared for the third time, the donkey gave up. This time the lane was so narrow there was room for an angel or a donkey, but not both, so the donkey lay down and Balaam hit it again.

This time, God gave the donkey a bit of help. The bit of help was speech.

"Excuse me!" said the donkey. "Will you stop hitting me?"

"Hit you!" said Balaam, who didn't seem surprised by a talking donkey. "You've been making me look like an idiot all day. I could kill you!"

"And do you think I'm doing this for fun?" demanded the donkey. "No? Then why do you think I *am* doing it?"

At last, Balaam saw the angel. He threw himself on his face before it in terror.

"About time!" said the angel. "Balaam, if you'd kept trying to go on, I would have killed you. Not the poor donkey, just you. Now, listen. Go to meet Balak but don't prepare to curse the Israelites. God will teach you what to say. Say only the words he gives you."

Now that the angel had made its point, it didn't trouble them any more. Balaam finally reached King Balak, who was delighted to see him.

"The Israelites are everywhere!" he said. "You can see some of them from here, and that's only a fraction of them. Just curse them, will you?"

"I can only say what God gives me to say," said Balak. He prayed, then spoke the words God gave him.

"I cannot curse these people because God doesn't curse them. He loves these people."

"*What?*" said Balak.

"It's what God told me to say," said Balaam.

"Come this way," said Balak. "Maybe the sight of all those Israelites is putting you off. I'll take you to a place where you can't see so many, and you can just curse a few of them."

But Balaam could only say the words God gave him.

"God has promised to bless these people," he said, "and he keeps his promises. Nothing can work against them. They are blessed, and everyone will be amazed at what…"

"Please!" said King Balak. "If you won't curse them, please will you stop blessing them?"

"I can only say what God gives me to say," said Balaam again.

"That's no good!" cried the king. "Can't you even curse them a little bit?"

Balaam looked down at the Israelites.

"These people are like a garden planted by God," he said. "Their kings will be powerful. Whoever blesses them will be blessed."

There was nothing Balak could do but send Balaam home. Perhaps, afterwards, he regretted sending for a man who would speak the truth. It was sure to cause trouble.

As for the donkey, it went home to a pleasant green field with no angels in it. It never said another word for the rest of its life.

As far as we know.

Hagar

Abraham and Sarah had an Egyptian slave girl, Hagar. This is her story.

THERE WERE THREE of us – Abraham, Sarah, and me – but it was all about Abraham and Sarah. I was only a slave.

Everyone respected Abraham. He spoke with God, and God blessed him and Sarah with everything they could want. All they still desired was a child, and God had promised them a son.

God had promised, but they'd been married for years without having children. Sarah grew too old. Finally she announced that if Abraham were going to have a son it couldn't be with her, so they'd settle for the next best thing. He'd have a baby with me.

You may find that shocking, but in those days a childless woman would "give" her slave girl to her husband to have a child. That's what being a slave meant – my body was hers to give. My child would be treated as hers. I wasn't asked to have Abraham's baby, I was told, and I always did as I was told. But my life changed the first time the baby kicked.

They could call it the promised child or Sarah's child, but I was the one

giving it life. I knew it was a boy, and every day I loved him more. Can you blame me for being happy? Can you blame me for thinking – *I'm having the baby, not you?* I couldn't help it.

I never openly disobeyed Sarah, but I learned to stand up to her. I had to, for the baby's sake. If she asked me to carry the heavy pails of water, I pointed out that I shouldn't lift anything heavy. Even when I was getting bigger she'd expect me to grind grain or cook all day in the hot sun, and that's too hard when you're pregnant. I needed rest, and Sarah hated that. She thought I was taunting her because I could have a baby and she couldn't. I couldn't ask for a pillow without Sarah thinking I was having a go at her.

She got her own back, though. She nagged, criticized, and blamed. Every moment of every day she did her best to make my life unbearable, and she succeeded. I never went to bed without tears. Abraham could have helped me – this was all about his baby! But no, he ignored all of Sarah's cruelty until I simply couldn't stand it. I ran away.

I had no idea where I was going. I just couldn't face another day with Sarah. Then before I'd gone far, something wonderful happened.

I didn't understand what was going on and I still find it hard to describe, but this was it. I was worn out and miserable, and I'd flopped down for a rest and a cry when I heard a voice.

It was a clear, strong voice, and kind. Was it God, or his messenger? I don't know, but I knew that Abraham and Sarah's God had something to say to me. Me, the runaway slave! In the kindest way he told me he cared about me, and I should go back. He would take care of me, and the baby would have his blessing.

I didn't know why their God cared about me, but he did. He made me strong enough to go back.

When Ishmael was born, I thought my heart would burst with love. Sarah could call him hers, but everyone knew he was my son, smiling up at Abraham with dark Egyptian eyes. Sarah treated him as her own, but I fed and cleaned him. It might have worked but for what happened next.

Sarah became pregnant. At her age! I couldn't believe it; she could hardly believe it herself. I didn't think she'd survive the birth, but she did, and so did her son, Isaac. I thought Abraham would never stop smiling. Even Sarah laughed!

Honestly, I was happy for them. At first Ishmael got upset, poor love, because suddenly Sarah wasn't interested in him any more, but he knew he had my love and that would never fail. In those days Abraham was still a good father, too. And my Ishmael was lovely with Isaac! If Isaac cried, Ishmael would run to rock the cradle or make him laugh. I loved that. Sarah didn't. Now that she had her own son, she couldn't bear the sight of mine. Ishmael had been her idea in the first place, but now there was only room for Isaac.

One day when Ishmael had been making Isaac laugh, Sarah flew into a rage. She raved at Abraham and told him that the "slave's brat" shouldn't be anywhere near Isaac. Ishmael and I had to leave. As simple as that.

I had given my life to that family. Abraham still loved Ishmael and didn't want us to go. But did he help us? Did he stand up to Sarah? He gave me a loaf of bread and a skin bag of water, put Ishmael into my arms, and told me God

would look after us. *Just as well,* I thought, *because you won't.* We walked away with Ishmael reaching out over my shoulder, sobbing and stretching out his arms to his daddy.

I'd never been far on my own. No wonder I got lost. We were in the wilderness, where everything looked the same. One loaf of bread and a skin bag of water doesn't go far in a hot dry wasteland with a hungry child.

I lost track of time. The water was finished. Ishmael, hot and heavy, became too weak even to cry and there wasn't a thing I could do to help him. When he began to burn with fever, I put him down in the shade of a bush and turned away because I couldn't bear to watch him die.

Then I heard the voice.

"Hagar, don't be afraid. God cares about you. Pick up your son. He has a future."

So their God was still with me! He must have been watching us, and he wasn't going to let us die in the desert.

I raised my head, though even that was a great effort. And there, not far away, was a well of clean water! It was cool and fresh and I carried it to my son, trickled it into his mouth and stroked it over his hot forehead. He opened his eyes and smiled right into my heart.

The God of Abraham saved us. Ishmael grew strong and skilful, and when the time came for him to marry I chose a wife for him, an Egyptian girl, like me. My God was the God of Abraham, but my people were my people.

Mephibosheth

Mephibosheth was the son of Jonathan, who was King Saul's son and David's best friend. He was a small child when his father died in battle.

MEPHIBOSHETH WAS KING Saul's grandson, and that was his problem. Saul had been the king of Israel but his mind had grown dark and afraid, so that he mistrusted the people nearest to him. Young, handsome David was the one all the people admired. Suspecting that David meant to seize the kingdom, Saul tried to kill him, and David fled for his life. Without David to lead the armies, the Israelites were defeated in battle by the Philistines, and Saul and Jonathan were killed. Soon, David became king.

Mephibosheth was only five years old, and all of Saul's family were afraid. David might want them all dead, so that none of them could claim the throne. Mephibosheth's nanny took action.

"If David doesn't kill him, the Philistines will," she said. "I have to get him to safety." She took the child in her arms and ran, with her long robe catching around her feet and the child growing heavy to carry. Rushing for safety, she stumbled, fell, and dropped Mephibosheth. His feet were so badly damaged that he was lame for the rest of his life, but she found him a safe place to grow up.

Many years later David sent for Ziba, who used to be Saul's servant, and asked him if anyone was still alive from Jonathan's family. He wanted to show them kindness for Jonathan's sake.

Ziba knew the answer. By this time Mephibosheth was grown up, married with a son, and living with friends. Ziba was sent to take him to David.

What was Mephibosheth to think? He had heard stories of David all his life. His nanny had been afraid of him. His grandfather had hated David. But his father and David had been best friends.

Maybe David really did just want to befriend him. Or maybe David wanted to keep Saul's grandson where he could see him so he couldn't rebel. All his life Mephibosheth had known how his nanny had carried him to safety, and it seemed that he still lived in the shadow of her fear, not knowing whom to trust.

He would much rather have stayed where he was, living quietly, but the king had sent for him. He had no choice but to go. At the splendid court of King David, he hobbled into the king's presence and bowed low.

"Great king," he said, "why am I here? Why should you take notice of me?

I'm worth no more to you than a dead dog!"

"Welcome, Mephibosheth, Jonathan's son!" said David. "All the land that belonged to Saul and Jonathan is yours now, and you will live here as a member of my family."

He sent for Ziba, who had found Mephibosheth and brought him to court.

"Ziba, long ago you served King Saul," he said. "Now, I want you to serve his grandson. I have given Mephibosheth all the lands that belonged to Saul. You and your family and servants are to farm it for him."

It was a long time since Ziba had served Saul, and he had been loyal to David ever since. What did he think about his family having to work for Mephibosheth? He had to obey the king's orders.

A time came when David's son Absalom turned against him and tried to seize the kingdom. David and his supporters were escaping from Jerusalem when Ziba came to meet them. He had brought two donkeys laden with bread, fruit, and wine for David and his followers.

"But where's Mephibosheth?" asked David. "Why hasn't he come to help me?"

"He stayed in Jerusalem, sir," replied Ziba. "Now that you've gone he's waiting to see if the people will make him king, as he's Saul's grandson."

David thought of all the kindness he'd shown Mephibosheth. There and then, angry and disappointed, he promised all Mephibosheth's lands to Ziba.

The rebellion failed, but to David's distress Absalom was killed and David came home heartbroken with grief for his son. Ziba and his servants rushed to escort David back to the city, and Mephibosheth, too, struggled out to meet him.

Mephibosheth looked wretched. His clothes and hair were unwashed and untidy and he looked as if he hadn't slept.

"Why didn't you come to help me?" demanded the king. "Where were you when I had to flee from my own city? Were you staying put, waiting for your chance?"

"Sir, Ziba tricked me!" cried Mephibosheth. "My lameness prevented me from coming to you, so Ziba said he'd take the supplies instead. Did he tell you that I had betrayed you? Your Majesty, he lied! Why would I desert you, when you've been so kind to me? But you are God's chosen king. Do whatever you will, and I will accept your judgment."

Either Mephibosheth was lying or Ziba was, and how could David tell which? But in his grief at the death of his son, he hardly cared.

"I don't want to hear any more of it," he said. "You and Ziba, divide the land between you."

"Great king!" cried Mephibosheth. "I don't care about the land! Let Ziba have it all! Why should I care, so long as you are home alive and well?"

So who was lying? Ziba or Mephibosheth?

Naboth's Vineyard

Ahab, king of Israel, married Jezebel, princess of Tyre. Jezebel made sacrifices to a god named Baal, and fought to make everyone else do the same. Elijah, God's prophet, had the courage to worship God and fight for justice.

ISRAEL'S LAWS MADE sure that God was honoured and the rights of ordinary people were respected, and Jezebel had no time for that. She expected the common people to do as they were told and she hated Elijah, who reminded Ahab that God was more important than royalty.

Near to Ahab's palace was a beautiful vineyard belonging to Naboth. The land had been in Naboth's family for generations, and grew excellent vines. The more Ahab saw of that vineyard the more he wanted it, so he offered to buy it from Naboth at a good price.

"Your Majesty, it's not for sale," said Naboth. "It's always been in my family, and I want to leave it to my children. I can't part with it for any money."

The king sulked. He went to bed and turned his face to the wall.

"My husband!" cried Queen Jezebel. "What has upset you?"

"Naboth won't sell me his vineyard," he muttered into his pillow.

"Are you the king or aren't you?" she demanded. "Leave it to me!"

Jezebel knew there were people who wanted to please the king enough to lie for him if they had to. She planned Naboth's death.

Blasphemy, which means cursing God, was seen as such a serious crime that it carried a death sentence. So did speaking or working against the king, which was treachery. Two people claimed in public that they had heard Naboth blaspheme and speak against the king, and these lies were enough to have Naboth found guilty. He was put to death by stoning. Jezebel went to the king, who was still sulking.

"How terrible!" she said. "Naboth was found guilty of blasphemy and treachery and he's been stoned to death! Quite right, too. And because he was a blasphemer and a traitor, his lands are yours now. Get up, and go to see your vineyard!"

Did Ahab suspect anything? If he did, he didn't ask questions. He took over the vineyard, but soon he had to face the anger of Elijah.

"What sort of king are you?" demanded Elijah. "Not content with murdering Naboth, you take over his property as well! You've always done what was wrong in God's sight, and that will bring disaster upon you and your kingdom!"

After that, Ahab bitterly regretted what he had done. But three years later he again ignored the advice of a prophet, went into battle, and was killed. Jezebel was thrown to her death from a window by people who had always hated her arrogance and injustice.

It was a high price to pay for a vineyard.

The Widow

Elisha was one of the great prophets of the Old Testament. This story shows his care for people in need.

I STOOD BEFORE THE prophet with my boys beside me. Seth was too old to hold my hand, or thought he was, but Nathan held on tightly and looked up at Elisha with big round eyes. He must have been afraid of the prophet with his bald head and long beard. I certainly was, though I knew he was a good man. Even the king feared Elisha.

Elisha was God's prophet and I'd heard that he could be fierce, but he was my only hope. I curtsied to him and the boys bowed. Nathan's little hand in mine was as thin as a claw. What sort of a mother lets her boys go hungry? One with no food left in the house and no money to buy any. I pressed my hand against my stomach to stop it from rumbling.

"My husband was a prophet, too, sir," I said. "He died not long ago."

"I remember him," he said. "How can I help you?"

I leaned closer to the prophet and whispered. The boys mustn't hear this.

"My husband borrowed money," I told him. "Now the lender wants it paid

back, and as my husband is now dead, there's no income. I begged the lender to be merciful, but he says if I can't pay it, he'll…" I forced out the terrible words, "… he'll take the boys and sell them as slaves."

I bit my lip hard and squeezed my eyes shut. In law, if I didn't repay the money, the lender had the right to take our home, our possessions, and even us to sell. My little boys could be dragged away and sold to strangers. Elisha was our last hope.

I don't know what I wanted him to do for us – work a miracle? Lend me the money? Reason with the lender? Nobody else could help.

He looked at the boys. Their cheekbones stood out, making their eyes look huge.

"What do you have at home?" he asked.

I nearly said "nothing", but then I thought of my last jar of oil. It was only a little one.

"A small bottle of olive oil," I said. "Nothing else."

"Go around to your friends," he said. "Ask if they can let you have any empty jars. Then take the children home, shut the door, and start pouring oil into the jars. When a jar is full, put it to one side and start on the next."

It didn't make sense. Filling a lot of jars from one small one was impossible! But I'd run out of possible things. If a prophet asked me to do the impossible, I'd do it.

The boys helped. They liked being useful, and it took their minds off their aching stomachs. We collected armfuls of jars, shut the door, and set to work. Seth brought me a jar and I filled it brimful with oil. He brought another and soon that was full too.

Then another and another – Nathan was laughing. My little jar was made of clay so I couldn't see how much oil was left. It just kept coming! Seth put one more jar in front of me, and I filled it.

"Next?" I said.

"That's the last one," he said. Rows and rows of jars covered the floor. Seth and I started to laugh, too.

I ran to find Elisha, and when I told him what had happened, he wasn't surprised.

"Take the oil and sell it," he said. "It'll pay the debt and leave enough money for your family to live on."

So, giving thanks to God, that's what we did. It was excellent oil, and we got a very good price for it. That night we had the first proper meal we'd eaten in weeks. As Elisha had promised, the money was enough to pay the debt and keep us until the boys and I had rebuilt our lives and could earn our living. And to this day, there's never been another drop of oil from that jar.

Naaman's Servant

Naaman (pronounced "Nayman") commanded the king of Syria's armies, and the king valued him highly. The Israelite girl telling this story was taken captive in a battle between Israel and Syria.

IF YOU WANT TO know anything, ask a servant. We know. But it's important to ask the right servant, because some of them can't be trusted.

I was a little girl when I was caught and taken to Syria, and I cried for a week. Mrs Naaman was kind to me, took me in, and trained me to be her maid – I think I'm about thirteen now. She treats me well and I'm never, ever beaten, and when the doctor told us about Naaman's illness I felt desperately sorry for her.

He said that terrible word and I was shocked, because saying "leprosy" was almost like swearing. Do you know about leprosy? It makes your body fail and die, slowly. What's worse, lepers aren't allowed to go near anyone else in case they pass it on. Imagine having to stay away from all your family and friends. You can't hug someone you love. You can't go to a party or a market; you can only mix with other lepers. Naaman had leprosy.

The king paid for doctors and medicines, but nothing worked. Then one morning when I was doing my mistress's hair, I was thinking out loud.

"I wish we were in Israel," I said. "There's a holy man there called Elisha, and he's a great servant of God. He can heal by God's help. I'm sure he could make my master well."

I'd hardly put her hairbrush away before she was organizing us. She sent messengers to the king, told me to pack, and took us all to Israel. Our king thought we should visit the king of Israel, not Elisha, and sent us to the palace with cartloads of gifts and money.

The king of Israel was shocked! He thought someone was trying to play a trick on him. Finally it was all sorted out and off we went to Elisha's house.

Elisha's servant Gehazi came out to meet us and took a message in to the prophet. We all waited outside, wondering what would happen. It was exciting, and a bit frightening. But Elisha didn't even come to the door! He just sent Gehazi out with a message:

"Tell Naaman to swim in the River Jordan. Seven times."

Naaman was furious. "Swim in the Jordan!" he thundered. "We've got better rivers at home – the Abana, the Pharpar – better than the Jordan! If I'm going to wash in a river, I'll choose a decent one!"

It was up to the servants to calm him down. We pointed out that if Elisha had asked him to do something difficult, he would have done it. So it wouldn't do any harm just to have a swim in the Jordan, would it? So he did, and by the time he'd dipped in and out of the river seven times his skin was as clear

and smooth as a child's! He offered Elisha money and presents as a reward but Elisha didn't want anything.

"Then please grant me one more thing," asked Naaman. "Let me take some earth home from this country, so that I can worship the God of Israel for the rest of my life."

Elisha gave him what he wanted. We were on our way home when Gehazi came running after us. All out of breath, he told us that some visitors had arrived unexpectedly and Elisha had sent him to ask for money to buy them food.

Naaman was glad to give it, but that wasn't the end of the story. We found out later that Gehazi had been lying. There were no visitors. He wanted the money for himself, and Elisha was furious when he found out.

Poor Gehazi. Last I heard of him, he was ill. He had leprosy.

Ebedmelech

*Ebedmelech was a servant in the royal palace in Jerusalem. This was not his country.
His dark skin marked him as a foreigner. He was a eunuch. No man would call him
a man, and no woman would care for him. Ebedmelech knew what it was to be left out,
rejected, and bullied. And he knew an honest man when he saw one.*

W AS THERE EVER a worse time for Jerusalem?
　　The army of Babylon surrounded the city and besieged it. Nobody
could go in, nobody could leave. No food or drink could be taken into
Jerusalem, and what the people had was running out. Even the wells were
running dry.

　　Jeremiah the prophet had always warned the king not to rebel against
the king of Babylon. The king had ignored him and rebelled anyway, and
now the Babylonians were starving them into surrender. Even now, Jeremiah
insisted: "God has told me that the Babylonians will be merciful to anyone who
surrenders to them. There will be no mercy for those who resist."

　　King Zedekiah refused, though the people cried out for bread.

　　"God is on our side," he said. "We will not surrender. God's Temple is here,

and God will not let anything happen to his Temple."

All his advisers told him he was right. But in the streets, in the Temple, and to the king himself, the prophet Jeremiah spoke a different message.

"Do you really think God will protect you just because you're his people?" he demanded. "You make sacrifices to other gods, you ignore God's prophets, you set your slaves free and then immediately make them slaves again. You seem to think that just because you have the Temple, you'll be safe. You are taking God for granted!

"There is hope for the people of Israel. There will be blessing. But it won't come from sitting here expecting God to rescue you from the Babylonians! God has shown me that they'll treat us kindly if we surrender to them."

The king didn't believe this and didn't want to hear it. He kept Jeremiah closely guarded. His advisers wanted Jeremiah silenced, and at last the king handed him over to them.

"Oh, do what you like," he told his advisers. "I can't be bothered with him. How can I stop you?"

The advisers didn't kill Jeremiah. They only took him outside and lowered him down an old well. There was no water in there, only deep, thick mud. Slowly, Jeremiah began to sink.

The news of what had been done to Jeremiah reached Ebedmelech. Appalled, he went straight to the king.

"Jeremiah is a good man, and your people have thrown him down the well!" he cried. "They've left him there to sink into the mud and die!"

Zedekiah regretted telling his advisers that they could do what they liked. The death of a prophet was a serious business,

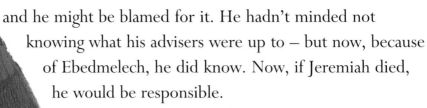

and he might be blamed for it. He hadn't minded not knowing what his advisers were up to – but now, because of Ebedmelech, he did know. Now, if Jeremiah died, he would be responsible.

"Take some men and get him out," he ordered. Before doing anything else, Ebedmelech ran down to a room where old clothes were kept. With a few friends, this bundle of rags, and some ropes, he ran to the well where Jeremiah felt the cold, squelching mud around his ankles, his knees, his waist.

"We're here, Jeremiah," he called down, and his voice echoed in the depths. "Can you hear me? I'm going to lower a rope with some rags tied to it. Put the ropes under your arms but use the rags as padding, so the ropes don't hurt you when we haul you up."

Foul-smelling mud clung and sucked around Jeremiah's ankles, but at last he was free. As soon as King Zedekiah knew about it, he sent for the prophet.

"Surrender the city," said Jeremiah. "If you don't, it will be destroyed."

But he knew what would happen. The king would remain stubborn, and the city would fall with terrible suffering and destruction. But Jeremiah spoke to Ebedmelech.

"Don't be afraid," he said. "You will not fall into the hands of the enemy. Whatever people may think about you, you were faithful to me when nobody else would stand by me, and our God will stand by you. You will live, and have a future."

Elizabeth

Elizabeth was related to Mary, the mother of Jesus. Her son John would be the one who prepared the way for Jesus' ministry.

OUR PEOPLE HAVE an old story about Abraham and Sarah, our ancestors. All the Jewish people are descended from them. The thing is, Sarah didn't become pregnant until she was ninety years old! She overheard an angel telling Abraham that she'd have a baby and she laughed so hard she fell over. I know how she felt.

My husband Zechariah was a priest. He'd been to the most holy place in the Temple for a solemn ceremony, and when he came home I could see from his face that something had happened. He was deathly pale, and looked as startled as a shocked cat. He put his fingers over his mouth, shook his head, and finally held out his hands and mouthed, "I can't speak!"

So he'd had a shock and lost his voice? I was ready to be sympathetic, to sit him down with a drink of water and get him to take deep breaths. But he wouldn't sit down, he wouldn't calm down, then he –

I tried to tell myself it wasn't funny. He dropped down to his knees, put

his hands together, then jumped up again, and flapped his arms, so he must have been desperate to tell me something. I put my hands over my mouth and bit my lip, but it was no good. He wasn't pleased, but the more he glared the more I laughed. I couldn't help it. He pointed to my stomach.

What did that mean? Why did he make that gesture? Did he mean I was putting on weight? I wanted to say, "What a nerve!" but I was laughing so hard I couldn't put two words together any more than he could. Then he did the "rocking the baby" action, and that stopped me.

We didn't talk about that. We had no child, and I was too old to have any hope of one. It was our quiet grief, the thing we never talked about. Pointing at me like that, doing that action – that was cruel.

"Are you blaming me for not having a child?" I demanded.

He shook his head furiously, then repeated the whole mime thing. Prayer. Something with wings. Baby. Me. It reminded me of Sarah's story – a childless woman, a message from God, a baby – but I wasn't Sarah, and it upset me.

Before very long I felt off-colour and I couldn't drink milk. Couldn't bear even the smell of it. But olives, though – I couldn't get enough of them! And as the weeks went by, and Zechariah still couldn't speak, I came to understand that he had received a message from God that day; and God keeps his word. I was growing rounder every day! I had a feeling it was a boy, and the name "John" was in my head, even though there wasn't anyone called John in my family or Zechariah's.

It was six months later, and the baby was moving, when I had the dream. I saw a glorious figure almost too bright to look on, but I could see the shape of wings. My husband's story slipped into my head and I thought I would see him, too, but I didn't. The figure kneeling before the angel wasn't Zechariah – it was my little cousin Mary. "Little cousin Mary!" She'd always be little Mary to me but she was old enough now to be married. Mary had been the nearest I ever had to a daughter, and I loved her.

I heard the angel tell Mary of the baby she would bring into the world, and in my dream I understood as I had never understood anything in my life before. It was as if Mary and I were part of a perfect pattern, or a dance, or a song

blended together in many parts. I didn't know how it all worked, but it did, and that was all I needed.

"Mary?" I said when I woke up, because the dream had been so vivid that I thought I was still with her. I was in my own bed beside Zechariah, and my baby was kicking so hard that I gave a little shriek, not of pain, but of surprise. Zechariah woke up and pulled a puzzled sort of face that I think meant, "Are you all right?"

"Oh, yes!" I said. "The baby just told me that Mary's coming to stay." And his little cousin, I thought, but I didn't tell Zechariah that. Zechariah yawned and went back to sleep.

Soon after that came a morning when my baby must have been having a wonderful time. He was doing somersaults! It was as if he was dancing for joy, and it could only mean one thing. I ran out – well, waddled out – and was halfway down the hill when I saw Mary running to meet me. Not my little cousin any more, but a young woman with a place at the centre of God's pattern. We hugged, we laughed, we wept for joy, and we sang.

The world can still hear us.

Centurion

A centurion was an officer in charge of a hundred men. This centurion was part of the army occupying Galilee, and was based in Capernaum.

I'M HAPPY TO tell you what happened, but I don't understand why it surprised everyone.

Tertius Gallus, centurion of Rome, posted in Galilee. When I say that, most soldiers make jokes about it. Almost as much trouble as Britain, they say, but warmer. I like Galilee, though.

Rome is the occupying power in this land, and you can't walk into somebody's country, take it over, and expect them to like you. You have to give them good reasons to like you, so I don't bully people – I get to know them.

I like their religion. They believe in one God, not dozens of them, and they're always having festivals. They have some great stories about their ancestors. Their meeting house is called a synagogue and this town didn't have one, so I built one for them. Best thing I could have done. I was glad to help them.

I treat my servants well, too. I look after them and expect the best out of

them, and we're all happy. They're a good team. Most of them have been with me for years. Lucius worked for my family when I was a boy, and when he became seriously ill it was like watching my own brother suffer.

It got worse. He was paralysed. I watched him lying there trying to speak. Then word came to the new synagogue, and from the synagogue through the streets, and from the streets it came in through the door of my house – the news that Jesus of Nazareth was not far away.

I'd heard about him. Everybody was talking about him; you'd have to be deaf not to hear about Jesus of Nazareth, and then you'd still hear about him because he'd heal you. He made blind people see and lame people walk. Nobody knew how it worked, it just did – and that was good enough for me. As a soldier, I knew authority when I heard about it. He had authority.

I didn't go to him myself. I'm what they call a Gentile, a non-Jew, and however well I got on with the Jews, I wasn't one of them. I asked some of my friends from the synagogue to take a message to him, asking him to do something for Lucius.

I was bending over Lucius's bed trying to get a few sips of water into his mouth when a slave ran through the house to tell me that Jesus was on his way. I hadn't intended Jesus to come all the way here! Why should he want to come to a Gentile house? I knew he could heal, and that was good enough for me. If he had the power to do that, he could do it anywhere.

"Go to meet him," I told the slave. "Take him a message. Tell him this – 'Lord, I'm not worthy to receive you in my home. I know a bit about power. I'm a centurion – I have to do what my senior officers tell me and my soldiers and servants have to do as I say. I understand about giving and receiving orders. If you say the word, Lucius will be healed.'"

I knew he'd received my message. I knew it the moment Lucius sat up and told me he felt better than he'd ever felt in his life.

I found out afterwards that Jesus really liked my message. He said he was impressed that I had so much faith in him, believing that he could heal without being there. Of course he could! He was a healer. His God had given him power and authority.

I pray to his God now. I hope it's all right for a Gentile to do that. I wish I could ask Jesus. I hope I meet him one day, face to face, to thank him. I've a feeling I will.

The Servants in the Courtyard

Jesus was arrested in the middle of the night, and put on trial at the High Priest's house. Peter wanted to see what would happen, but was terrified of being arrested.

THEY BROUGHT A man to the High Priest's house in the middle of the night. They don't normally do that.

I was in charge of the maidservants and one of them was Debbie. Debbie was new, young, and very annoying. She was always wanting my attention, always coming to tell me things – a chattering little busybody. She knew she mustn't run on duty, but she walked so fast she looked like a busy little duckling. She came bustling in to find me.

"Please, Mrs Annie, you know the man they just brought in?"

"No," I said. I did know, but I didn't want to, especially not from Duckling Debbie.

It was like this. All of a sudden, at night when it should have been quiet, a lot of visitors had arrived. Most of them were priests, and the council and the

elders turned up too. Any fool could see what that meant. Something big was going to happen, something that involved all the leaders of our community holding a meeting that they couldn't hold in daylight, or in public. I realized what it was about when the guards dragged Jesus of Nazareth in.

They were going to put Jesus on trial there and then, at the High Priest's house at night. It was illegal, but to tell you the truth, I thought, *Jesus of Nazareth has asked for this.* Whenever he was around, trouble started. Only on Sunday he'd come riding into the city on a donkey just like the king in the Scriptures and there'd almost been a riot. A quiet arrest and trial at night might be illegal, but it would sort him out. If that was what they wanted to do, I chose not to know about it. When silly Debbie came blabbing to me, I didn't want to hear.

"Only," she said, "there's one of his friends outside. I asked him and he said he doesn't know Jesus, but he's lying, I know, 'cause I've seen them together. They're best mates, him and Jesus. Shouldn't he be arrested too?"

Probably, I thought, but it was nothing to do with me. And I certainly wasn't going to jump to attention whenever little Debbie came telling tales.

"He's from the north," she went on. "You can tell by the way he talks. He even talks like Jesus."

For heaven's sake, it was Passover! North, south, east, west, everyone was in Jerusalem!

"I think we should all mind our own business and get on with our work, Debbie," I said coldly. She wiggled off, pouting like a toddler, and I went on filling the oil lamps. I could hear angry voices from the room where they'd taken Jesus. Soon Debbie was back, having found another maid even sillier than she was.

"We've *both* heard him!" gushed Debbie. "Please, Mrs Annie, you have to go and listen! He's Galilean! Susie says she's seen him with Jesus. His name's Peter. He says he's nothing to do with Jesus, but I'm sure he's lying."

"Do you girls have no work to do?" I snapped. They vanished without another word.

I'd have to sort this out. I'd find out who this man was, and if he did turn out to be Jesus' friend I'd call the guards and get him arrested. As I strode out of the door, I heard Debbie whispering to her friend, "She's angry! We shouldn't have crossed her!"

I nearly turned and gave her a tongue-lashing, but I didn't. That word "crossed" had stopped me.

Cross. If Jesus was found guilty, it would be the Romans who put him to death – and that's what he'd get. I thought Jesus should be stopped, but to die on a cross? I wouldn't want that to happen to anyone, not my worst enemy.

I went out to the courtyard. The big, tall man was sitting there with the servants swarming around him, taunting him and asking questions – "Are you from Galilee? You are, aren't you? You were with Jesus. Go on, say something!"

It was horrible, like seeing flies gathering around a leper. He was afraid and out of his depth and wanted to be anywhere else but here. I clapped my hands.

"What do you think this is, a fairground show?" I demanded. "Do you people have

work to do, or shall I ask the guards to help you?"

That sorted them out. Nobody wanted to be on the wrong side of the guards.

"And you," I said to the man, "Out. Now."

The sun was rising. I heard the cock crow. The crowd cleared away. The man got up, slowly, wearily, and at that moment the soldiers led Jesus of

Nazareth across the yard. Their eyes met. There was already a big purple bruise on Jesus' face, and he didn't get that by accident. I looked away.

When Jesus had gone I looked around for the tall man, but he'd taken my advice and was heading out of the gate. That was where I found him later, leaning against a wall, sobbing his heart out.

When I'd told him to get out, I'd meant him to get a lot further away than this. No friend of Jesus was safe here.

"I told you to go," I said.

He turned to look at me and his face was wet with tears.

"I let him down," he whispered. "They asked me, and I lied! I disowned him!"

"Go!" I said, and walked briskly back to the house to sort the girls out. I couldn't afford to be seen talking to a friend of Jesus.

Dorcas

After Jesus' resurrection, his friends the apostles led the church. This is a story from that time about Dorcas, who lived in Joppa.

I LOVED JESUS BEFORE I knew about him, because I loved the poor. There were so many of them in Joppa. They weren't lazy or bad, just poor. They needed kindness.

Sewing is one of the things I've always been good at, and I enjoy it. The poor people in Joppa wore their few clothes until they were worn to rags; the children wore the same things until they were bursting out of them, and in winter they were cold to the bone. So I sewed for them. If you make a boy a warm coat, it's like wrapping him in a hug that will last all winter. Give a woman a well-fitting dress and she'll walk taller and hold up her head.

It was too much for me to do alone, so I got my friends to help. We wanted the best for the poor, not plain, cheap garments. We sewed bright colours for the children, with oversewn seams that would last and tucks so they could be let out or taken in.

It was going very well until I caught some nasty little infection, which suddenly became quite bad. Soon, I was too ill to do anything but go to bed and rest. Breathing became hard work. It was a struggle to draw the next breath, and the next.

Then suddenly everything was simple and beautiful. There was no pain, only light and the smile of Jesus, who stood before me.

My friends carried me to an upstairs room and I lay soaking up those lovely moments. But although I was sure I was in heaven, I could hear everything happening in the house. Downstairs, my friends were wailing and crying and sending someone to find Jesus' friend Peter, who was not far away. I wanted to tell them not to cry. Jesus was smiling down on me. Why should they cry?

When Peter came into the house, I felt a change before I heard anything. I could feel that somebody with authority was near, someone very close to the heart of Jesus. Then, what a fuss! My friends were following him up the stairs and all talking at once – "Sir, she made this beautiful dress for a little girl, sir, she made this lovely wool cloak, look at the little baby clothes and the embroidery, how neat…"

Poor Peter! I could picture them all holding up baby clothes, turning them inside out so he could see the stitching, and his not knowing what to make of it. Tucks and embroidery – what did that mean to a fisherman? Then only Peter was there, on his knees by my bed, holding my hand. I heard the prayer of a tired and confused man.

"What am I to do, Lord?" he prayed. "I don't understand. All those women downstairs crying and flapping clothes at me and I don't know what to do! They seem to think I can raise Dorcas from the dead. Is that what you want? I saw you raise people from the dead. I saw you yourself, after you came back. I know you can do that through me, if that's what you want. But is it? People died every day; you didn't bring them all back. Is there something Dorcas still needs to do? Here I am, Lord. Raise her if you will."

I looked at the face of Jesus. I saw the smile that I know is still waiting for me.

"Not yet," he said.

The vision vanished. I was back. Peter helped me up, but I didn't need it. I was on my feet and as nimble as a ten year old.

"Thank you," I said, though part of me felt I'd rather be back in that heavenly light.

"Thank Jesus, not me," said Peter. "Shall we go back to your friends?"

So we did, but he didn't stay long.

We both had work to do.

Eunice

We know little about Eunice, but she played an important role in the early church.
She was a friend of Paul.

I'M EUNICE, AND I live with my mother, Lois, and my son, Timothy, so you could say I'm the one in the middle. I'm probably a bit like your mother, if your mother is always trying to keep an eye on an elderly parent and her almost grown-up son at the same time.

Excuse me a moment – *Mother, are you all right? Are you warm enough?*

I grew up in a traditional Jewish family, but we lived in Greece. My father died young, but Mother made sure that I learned all the Jewish stories – Abraham, Isaac, Joseph and his brothers, Ruth; I soaked them all up. Every Friday night we had our special family meal for the beginning of the sabbath. I was a real daughter of the Hebrews but we lived in a Greek city and most of my friends were Greek, so was it any surprise that I fell in love with a Greek? Was it any surprise that I married him?

Oh yes, it was. Mother was appalled. Jewish girls weren't supposed to marry "out". I always felt that I lived in two worlds but didn't belong to either of them, though I knew I belonged with Leon.

The day my son Timothy was born, Mother held him in her arms and said with great satisfaction, "My little Jewish grandson!" Jewish inheritance is passed through the mother, so any child of mine would be Jewish. Timothy grew up with Mother and I telling him our Jewish stories and Leon teaching him Greek myths, Greek philosophy, Greek songs.

It was somebody in the Jewish community who told us about Paul, who was speaking about the new kind of faith every day, but not in the synagogue. Paul would speak in the middle of town or anywhere. Mother heard him first and told us that we had to meet him, but I wasn't keen. I was afraid that this was some loudmouth who'd look down on Leon for not being Jewish. But I went. We all went together.

We stood around with the rest of the crowd, and heard Paul speak. I can't remember everything he said that day, but I remember these words that struck right to my heart and gave me hope. He said:

"If you belong to Jesus Christ, there are no barriers between you anymore. There's no more 'I'm a Jew and you're a Greek', or 'I'm free and you're a slave'. It doesn't matter if you're male or female. We all belong to Christ, and that's what matters."

When I heard that, I wanted Christ, this welcoming Jesus Christ who didn't care whether you were Jewish or Greek. We all learned from Paul and became part of the Christian community, and it was like being set free.

Paul became a great friend to our family, and after Leon died, Paul became the person Timothy looked up to. Time passes too quickly, and Timothy's almost grown up now, getting ready to go with Paul on his next journey. How do I feel about that?

I'm proud of Timothy. I'm thankful for his faith and I want him to take his place in the world. I just wish he could do it without going away because I don't know how I can bear that. I don't know if he's ready for this. He's shy, he needs confidence. And I don't even know how long this journey will last. You never know with Paul. When will I see Timothy again? When will I even hear from him? But this isn't all about me, is it?